Animal Studies

STUDENT ACTIVITY BOOK

SCIENCE AND TECHNOLOGY FOR CHILDREN®

NATIONAL SCIENCE RESOURCES CENTER
Smithsonian Institution • National Academy of Sciences
Arts and Industries Building, Room 1201
Washington, DC 20560

NSRC

The National Science Resources Center is operated by the Smithsonian Institution and the National Academy of Sciences to improve the teaching of science in the nation's schools. The NSRC collects and disseminates information about exemplary teaching resources, develops and disseminates curriculum materials, and sponsors outreach activities, specifically in the areas of leadership development and technical assistance, to help school districts develop and sustain hands-on science programs.

STC Project Supporters

National Science Foundation
Smithsonian Institution
U.S. Department of Defense
U.S. Department of Education
John D. and Catherine T. MacArthur Foundation
The Dow Chemical Company Foundation
E. I. du Pont de Nemours & Company
Amoco Foundation, Inc.
Hewlett-Packard Company
Smithsonian Institution Educational Outreach Fund
Smithsonian Women's Committee

This project was supported, in part,
by the
National Science Foundation
Opinions expressed are those of the authors
and not necessarily those of the Foundation

ISBN 0-89278-962-X

Published by Carolina Biological Supply Company, 2700 York Road, Burlington, NC 27215.
Call toll free 800-334-5551.

This material is based upon work supported by the National Science Foundation under Grant No. ESI-9252947. Any opinions, findings, and conclusions or recommendations expressed in this material are those of the author(s) and do not necessarily reflect the views of the National Science Foundation.

CB787470109

Contents

Introduction

"Home, sweet home."

Did you ever hear this phrase? What does it mean?

Animals know what this means, even if they can't say it in words. After you finish this unit, you will know, too.

You will care for and study three small animals.

One lives in water.
One lives on land and in water.
One lives on land.

You'll learn that all animals need certain things in order to grow and live.
But animals are also different; each needs different amounts of these basic things.

Each animal depends on other animals. It also depends on the plants that live around it.
Together, these things make up an animal's habitat.

Scientists study animals in their habitats.
They watch the animals over long periods of time.

In this unit, you will watch your frog, crab, and snail.
Do you think that an animals' behavior is related to its habitat?

Finally, what about you?
You're an animal, too.
How is your "home, sweet home" different from an animal's home?
How is it the same?

Keep your science notebook handy during this unit.
Record your predictions, observations, and results.
Use it when you discuss your ideas with your classmates.
At the end of the unit, review your notes. See how much you've learned!

Thinking about Animals and Their Homes

Think and Wonder

How do animal scientists learn about animals? You will be studying a frog, a crab, and a snail. How would you go about studying them? Right now, think about how these three animals are alike. How are they different? What would they need to survive in your classroom?

Materials

For you

    1 pencil

    1 science notebook

    1 copy of **Record Sheet 1-A: Studying Animals**

For you and your partner

    1 *Animal Studies* Student Activity Book

Find Out for Yourself

1. In this unit, you will study three animals. Listen as your teacher describes what you will learn.

2. Put today's date on the first page of your science notebook. You will use your notebook to record your ideas and observations. Be sure to date each new entry. Record only one entry per page.

3. What do you think you know about frogs, crabs, and snails? Write your thoughts about each animal in your notebook.

4. Now share your thoughts with the class. Your teacher will record your ideas.

5. Discuss these questions with your group:

   - In what ways do you think frogs and crabs are similar? Frogs and snails? Crabs and snails?

   - In what ways do you think frogs and crabs are different? Frogs and snails? Crabs and snails?

   - In what ways do you think each animal's life is similar? Different?

6. Share your group's thoughts with the class.

7. Respond in your notebooks to these questions:

   ■ Where do you think scientists study animals?

   ■ What are some ways you think scientists study animals?

   ■ Where can you go in this area to observe animals in their natural homes?

8. Think about what you will need to do to prepare for bringing frogs, crabs, and snails into the classroom. Then fill out **Record Sheet 1-A: Studying Animals.**

9. Give the record sheet to your teacher.

Ideas to Explore

1. Think about having a pet. What makes a good pet? What do you need to know about a pet before you can bring it home? Why are some animals pets and not others?

2. Find out what types of pets your classmates have. Then make a bar or picture graph showing the results. Share your graph with the class. Which graphs are easiest to read? How could you use each graph?

3. Do you have a pet at home? Write a short paragraph about it. Why did you choose that animal? What do you need to do to keep it healthy and give it a good home?

4. How could your class attract animals to your schoolyard? Brainstorm some ideas with your class. You and your class can study the schoolyard animals at the same time you study the animals in your classroom.

Inviting Animals into the Classroom

Think and Wonder

Look around you. What are the living and nonliving things in your school? Observing the school will help you plan a home for the dwarf African frog, fiddler crab, and land snail. What does each animal need to survive?

Materials

For you
- 1 pencil
- 1 science notebook
- 1 **Record Sheet 1-A: Studying Animals**

For you and your group
- 1 piece of white drawing paper or poster paper
- 1 **Animal Background**

Find Out for Yourself

1. Look around the room. What living things do you observe? What nonliving things?

2. Share your observations with the class. Help your teacher put the observations in groups.

3. Discuss some other places in or around your school where you spend part of the day. Later, on your own, observe some of these places. Record your observations in your notebook. Be prepared to share your observations in a later lesson.

4. Look at **Record Sheet 1-A.** Discuss these questions with the class:

   - What do you need to know to bring frogs, snails, and crabs into the classroom to live?

   - How could you find information about each animal?

   - Where could you go to study frogs, crabs, and snails?

5. Study the picture of your group's animal in its natural home. Read below the picture to find out more. Then talk with your group. How could you help your animal survive in the classroom?

6. How will your group work together? Sometimes, members of a group have an extra job.

- **Moderator.** Keeps the group working, makes sure each member has a chance to give his or her ideas, and helps the group work together.

- **Reporter.** Tells the group's ideas to the whole class. For this activity, the reporter will read the **Animal Background** out loud to the group. Then the reporter will read to the class what the group has written about the animal habitat to the class.

- **Recorder.** Writes down any information that the group will tell the class. For this activity, the recorder lists what the group thinks should go in the animal's classroom home. The recorder may also draw what is inside the animal's home.

- **Investigator.** Ask the teacher questions that come up while the group is working. For this activity, the investigator will ask the teacher to explain any directions the group does not understand. The investigator also can look back at the **Animal Background** sheet to help the group complete its work.

Help your group decide each person's job.

7. Talk about these questions with your group:

- What items from the animal's natural home must also be in its classroom home?

- Think about the materials you can get from pet stores. Which of these materials do you think the animal's classroom home should contain? Why?

The recorder will write or draw your group's habitat proposal. The reporter should be ready to share the proposal.

8. Listen while each group describes its ideas for the animal's classroom home. Then hang up your proposal for other groups to see.

9. What things were the same, or "basic," in every group's animal home? Share your thoughts.

10. What things were different, or "special," in each home? Share your thoughts.

11. Look at the lists again. Use these ideas in the next lesson when you create a frog home.

Ideas to Explore

1. Think about your school environment. Are students singing? Is lunch cooking? Write a poem describing your school, using either all sounds or all smells.

2. How are a house cat and a tiger alike? Read a book such as *Cats: In from the Wild,* by Caroline Arnold.

3. Read a book about making homes for animals. Try *Habitats: Making Homes for Animals and Plants,* by Pamela Hickman.

4. Visit a zoo. What does the zookeeper include in each animal habitat? How has the zookeeper met each animal's basic needs? Can you find an animal that has special needs?

5. Read a book about different animal homes. Try *A Magic School Bus Hops Home*, by Joanna Cole.

Living in Water: Dwarf African Frogs

Think and Wonder

Today you will create a classroom home, or **habitat,** for the dwarf African frog. Think about how you will meet the frog's needs in the classroom. What living and nonliving things will you include in its habitat? What questions do you have about the frog?

Materials

For you
- 1 pencil
- 1 science notebook
- 1 hand lens
- 1 **Animal Log Checklist**

For you and your partner
- 1 dwarf African frog

For you and your group
- 1 large cup of gravel and lid
- 1 tank
- 4 elodea sprigs
- 1 china marker
- 1 metric ruler
- 1 small cup with green-dotted lid
- 1 teaspoon
- 1 piece of notebook paper
- 1 pail of conditioned tap water

Find Out for Yourself

1. Look at your frog habitat proposals from Lesson 2. Talk with your class about the important parts of the frog's home.

2. Your teacher has materials to make a water environment. How can you use these things to make your frog's classroom home? Discuss how each item should be placed in the frog's tank.

3. Turn to pgs. 14–15. Look and listen as your teacher goes over the instructions on how to set up the frog habitat.

4. Pay attention as your teacher shows you how to pick up your materials. The moderator needs to let the teacher know when your group is ready for the plants.

Figure 3-1

Distribution center

For each team of four students

1 LARGE CUP & LID · 1 TANK & LID · 1 SMALL CUP & LID · 2 CUPS of GRAVEL · 1 CHINA MARKER · 1 RULER · PAPER TOWEL · AND A PAIL OF WATER ➡ · 1 SPOON

5. Time to get to work. Remember to have your recorder list all the living and nonliving parts of the frog habitat.

6. Work until your group's habitat is complete. Have the moderator let the teacher know when you are done. Watch as your teacher adds two frogs to your habitat.

7. Keep the small plastic cups, lids, and spoons. Return the other materials to the distribution center.

8. Do you think your frog has everything it needs now to survive? Is anything missing? Discuss this with your class. Then follow these steps:

   ■ Pick up about half a small cup of frog food.

   ■ Write your group's letter beside the green dot on the habitat and on each item you have kept.

Figure 3-2

How to feed the frogs

Put a pinch of food on the water. Tap the food with the spoon until the frogs come over. Then sink some of the food with the spoon.

9. Look at Figure 3-2. Watch as your teacher shows you how to feed your frog.

10. Feed your frog. Talk about what you observed during the feeding.

   ■ What happened when you put food in the tank?

   ■ Did both frogs respond to the food? What happened when you moved the food with the spoon?

   ■ How much food was eaten?

   ■ Did the frogs eat from the surface or bottom of the habitat?

   Think about these questions each time you feed your frog.

11. Remember your list of living and nonliving things in the school? Help the class make a similar list for the frog habitat.

12. Listen as your teacher talks to you about how to care for your frog.

   ■ **Feeding schedule.** The frogs should be fed one or two times a day. If you see food in the tank, skip one of the feedings that day. If food is still in the tank the next day, you may be feeding your frog too much. Remove the extra food with a spoon so the food does not dirty, or contaminate, the water. Give your frog less food next time. If food sticks to the floating elodea, remove the elodea, rinse it with clean water, and put it back in the tank.

■ **Water.** You will need to refresh the water in the tank every two weeks (see Figure 3-3). To do this, use the large green-dotted plastic cups. Carefully remove two old cupfuls of water from the tank. Then replace the old water with two fresh cupfuls.

Figure 3-3

Replacing water in frog tanks

■ **Habitat placement.** Put your frog habitat in a place that does not get direct sunlight. Keep the habitat away from drafts and extreme heat.

13. Now that you have observed your dwarf African frogs, what questions do you have about them? Write your questions on the small paper your teacher will give you. Put your initials on the paper. Stick the paper on the big sheet of newsprint called "What We Would Like to Know about Our Frogs." You can keep adding questions as you study your frog more.

14. Your teacher will give you a copy of the **Animal Log Checklist.**

■ When do you think people would want to record observations about an animal?

■ What are some ways observations could be recorded?

Share your thoughts with the class. Then listen as your teacher tells you about a type of journal called a log.

15. You will make a list of questions to help you remember what to record in your log about each animal. What are some animal behaviors you might observe? As your teacher records questions, write them on your log checklist.

16. Make a section in your notebook for an animal log. Put your checklist in the front of that section. Title a page in the section "Frog."

17. Look at your checklist. Which behavior question can you answer about the frog? Record your observations in the log. Then check the box next to the question you have answered.

Ideas to Explore

1. Do some research. How are frogs and toads alike? How are they different?

2. Make a Venn diagram to compare the frog's natural habitat with the classroom habitat you just created.

3. Find the Congo and Zaire on a map of Africa. Research what other kinds of frogs might be found in the lakes and ponds of Central Africa. How about plants?

4. Find out what it means to "domesticate" an animal. Research the natural habitats of early dogs and cats.

Student Instructions for Building a Dwarf African Frog Habitat

1. Use a china marker to write the names of your team members near the top of the tank. This will be the front of your habitat.

2. Now use the china marker to mark a waterline 2.5 cm (1 in) below the top of the tank.

3. Add two cups of gravel.

4. Slope the gravel so the high end is in the back and the low end is in the front.

5. Cover the gravel with a piece of notebook paper.

6. Slowly add water to the middle of the tank until you reach the waterline mark. The water will hit the paper and not disturb the gravel.

7. Remove the paper and throw it away.

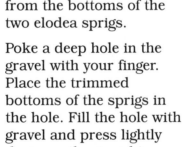

8. Remove the leaves for about 2.5 cm (1 in) up from the bottoms of the two elodea sprigs.

   Poke a deep hole in the gravel with your finger. Place the trimmed bottoms of the sprigs in the hole. Fill the hole with gravel and press lightly down on the gravel to anchor the sprigs.

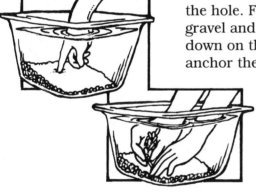

9. Float the two other elodea sprigs in the water.

Observing the Frogs More Closely

Think and Wonder

What is a scientific drawing? Why are they important? Today, you will make some drawings of the frog. You will record your observations in words, too. Plus, you will hold a science meeting. What do you think a science meeting is for?

Materials

For you

   1 science notebook
   1 **Record Sheet 4-A: Observing the Frog**
   1 **Record Sheet 4-B: Drawing the Frog**
   1 hand lens
   1 pencil

For you and your partner

   1 cup and lid
   1 dwarf African frog

For you and your group

   1 frog habitat
   1 spoon

Find Out for Yourself

1. Think about your frog observations so far. What characteristics of the frog should you focus on? Discuss your ideas with the class.

2. You will record today's frog observations on **Record Sheet 4-A.** You will write down the characteristics you observe in the first column of the record sheet.

3. You will draw your frog on **Record Sheet 4-B.** But first, talk with the class about these questions:

   ■ What do you think a scientific drawing is?

   ■ Have you ever seen scientific drawings of animals? Where?

- Why do you think scientific drawings of animals are made?

- How do you think they are used?

- In what ways do you think a drawing of the dwarf African frog will help you compare the frog with other animals?

- What should be included in a scientific drawing of the frog? How could **Record Sheet 4-A** help you?

4. Gather with your group around the frog habitat. Then collect your materials and get to work.

5. Have you and your partner finished both record sheets? Talk about your observations with the other pair in your group. Remember to add any new questions to the "What We Would Like to Know about Our Frogs" list.

6. Now, share your observations and drawings with the class. Discuss the answers to these questions:

- In what ways does having a drawing help you better understand the written descriptions of the frog's characteristics?

- Would a drawing alone give you enough information?

7. Put both record sheets back in your notebook and help clean up.

8. Take your notebook to the space for the science meeting. Listen as your teacher explains the reason for science meetings.

9. Talk with the class about some ways to answer your questions about the frog.

10. Pay attention as your teacher explains how you can use **Record Sheet 4-C: Science Discovery Sheet.**

Ideas to Explore

1. How is the frog like something you know? Complete these sentences:

   It moves like a _____.

   It is as big as a _____.

2. Do research on other kinds of frogs. How are they like the dwarf African frog? How are they different?

3. Make origami frogs with the class. Create a diorama for them. Your teacher can give you instructions.

Living Where Land and Water Meet: Fiddler Crabs

Think and Wonder

It's time to get your second animal—the fiddler crab. What do you think will go in the fiddler crab's habitat? How will you care for the fiddler crab? You will also read about dolphins. What do you know about how scientists study dolphins?

Materials

For you

    1 pencil

    1 science notebook

    1 hand lens

For you and your partner

    1 fiddler crab

For you and your group

    1 pail of water with lid

    1 large cup with lid

    1 tank

   4½ cups of sand-humus mixture

    1 china marker

    1 metric ruler

    1 small cup with lid

    1 teaspoon

    1 water bowl

    1 model of hairgrass

Find Out for Yourself

1. Discuss the "Habitat Information Table" with the class. Help identify the characteristics of the frog habitat. Which frog needs are met?

2. Look again at the crab habitat proposal from Lesson 2. Now that you have created a frog habitat, do you want to change the proposal at all?

3. Your teacher has some materials to create a crab habitat. How do they match the elements in your proposal? Share your thoughts with the class.

4. Turn to pgs. 22–23. Look and listen while your teacher goes over the instructions for creating the crab habitat. Help your group decide who will be the moderator, recorder, reporter, and investigator.

5. How do you pick up your materials for the crab habitat? Your teacher will show and tell you. What do you need to bring with you for the sand-humus mixture?

6. Remember, the group recorder will list every living and nonliving thing that goes in the habitat. Now pick up your materials and begin working.

Figure 5-1

Sample distribution center

7. When your group is ready, have the moderator ask the teacher to net you two crabs. Observe them carefully.

8. For now, keep the small plastic cups, lids, pails, and spoons. Return the other materials to the distribution center.

9. Do the crabs have what they need to survive in the classroom? Share your thoughts with the class. Then follow these steps:

   ■ Pick up about half a small cup of crab food.

   ■ Write your group's letter beside the orange dot on the habitat and each item you have kept.

10. Feed the crabs. Put a pinch of plankton on the land in your habitat. Also put a few pieces of plankton in the water. Then, discuss these questions with the class:

    ■ What happened when you put food in the tank?

    ■ Do the crabs respond to food the same way the frogs do?

■ How are the crabs' responses different?

11. Look at the circle your teacher has made. Listen as the group reporters talk about the elements in the crab habitats.

12. You will need to take extra good care of the crab habitats. Here's how:

■ **Feeding schedule.** Feed the crabs once a day. Take out any old food. Then add fresh food to both the land and water. You can put small pieces of apple, banana, or lettuce on the sand.

■ **Water.** Keep your group's water pail full of conditioned salt water. Know where the water conditioner and Instant Ocean™ will be kept. You will need to change the habitat's water once a week. Try not to spill any water on the sand!

■ **Temperature.** The crabs will be very active at a room temperature of about 15°C to 20°C (60°F to 68°F).

■ **Habitat placement.** Keep the crabs in a well-lit place. Keep them away from extreme heat and drafts. When the habitat needs to be moved, be sure to move it slowly and carefully.

13. What questions do you have about fiddler crabs? Write them on the small pieces of paper your teacher hands out. Put your initials on the papers. Tape the papers on the sheet "What We Would Like to Know about Our Crabs."

14. Write in your science notebook what you know about how people study dolphins.

15. Read "Diving into Dolphin Behavior" (pgs. 24–25).

16. When you are done reading, record in your notebook two or three things you have learned about how people study dolphins.

17. Share with the class what you learned from the reading. Then discuss these questions with the class:

■ How is the animal research you are doing similar to the dolphin research being done at the DRC? How is it different?

■ How is your animal log similar to the data sheet the DRC is using? How is it different?

18. Start a crab section in your animal log. Remember to use the checklist when you observe the crabs.

Ideas to Explore

1. Research other kinds of crabs. Create a crab display.

2. Make a Venn diagram to compare the fiddler crab's natural habitat with its classroom habitat.

3. Feed crabs some other foods. (You might try tuna, shrimp, green vegetables, and fruits.) What do they like?

4. Do you know what "crustaceans" are? Find out. Then research the nutritional value of crustaceans. What are some dishes that contain these animals?

Student Instructions for Building a Fiddler Crab Habitat

1. Use a china marker to write the names of your team members on the lid of the tank. Open the dial on the top of the lid so that air will get into the habitat.

2. Bring the tank bottom and large plastic cup to the distribution center. On one end of the tank, slowly add 4½ cups of the sand-humus mixture. Then return to your group.

3. Use the bowl to "bulldoze" a small amount of sand-humus to the opposite side of the tank from the sand-humus pile. Then leave the bowl in place. There should now be a pile of sand-humus— and not just an empty space—between the bowl and the end of the tank. Make the pile level with the bowl.

4. Now adjust the pile of sand-humus mixture opposite the water bowl against the end of the tank so that the mixture gradually slopes toward the bowl edge. Using the spoon, a pencil, or your finger, fill in the rest of the spaces between the bowl and the tank sides with the sand-humus mixture. The mixture should be even with all sides of the bowl.

5. With a ruler, measure the depth of the sand-humus mixture from the outside of the tank. Make sure the high end is at least 5 cm (2 in) deep.

6. Now plant the model hairgrass. Use the spoon to make a shallow hole in the low end of the sand-humus slope about 2.5 cm (1 in) from the bowl. Create a stand of "marsh grass."

7. Fill the water bowl halfway with salt water, using the large plastic cup. (It should be about 1.3 cm [½ in] deep.) Use your ruler to check the water depth. Be careful not to spill water onto the sand-humus.

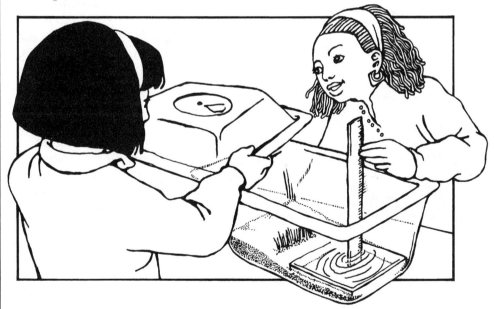

The habitat is now ready for your crabs. But, check the water level once a day because some water may evaporate. Remember to keep the water about 1.3 cm (½ in) deep at all times!

Important: You and your team will have to change the crabs' water at least once a week. So, each time you use up the extra salt water, you will need to make more. Your teacher will tell you how.

Diving into Dolphin Behavior

You are studying frogs and crabs. But there are places all over the world where scientists and other researchers study other animals, too. Let's read about a place that studies dolphins.

Welcome to the Dolphin Research Center (DRC), located in Grassy Key, in the Florida Keys. This is the home of a group of Atlantic bottlenose dolphins and the humans who study and care for them.

The staff already knew a lot about this type of dolphin. To learn even more, they talked to other dolphin experts. They read research findings on dolphins. They observed the dolphins' behavior over several years. And they recorded their observations, just like you're recording your frog observations in your animal log. Over a period of time, through observing the animals, the staff designed a habitat necessary to meet all the dolphins' needs and allow them to survive and reproduce.

After a while, one special behavior interested the staff members. They noticed that different mother dolphins raised their baby dolphins, called **calves,** in different ways. Some mothers spent all their time with their calves and nursed them for long periods of time. Other mothers spent less time with their calves and did not nurse them for very long. In other words, there were different mothering styles.

The staff began to wonder about this behavior. Did the type of mothering style affect when the calves were ready to feed on fish rather than only their mothers' milk? And how did the mothering style affect whether or not the calves survived?

The researchers decided to focus on these questions and began a two-year study on each new baby born at the DRC to try to find the answers. Why a two-year study? Because it takes time for the calves to grow up and separate from their mothers. A two-year study also enables the scientists to collect much information through observation.

about two years. The information that Amanda and Karen collect is called data.

What will they do with all this data? The research team will enter the data into a computer. The computer helps them analyze their data so they can answer their question about the calves' independence and the mothering styles. They will write papers and share the information with other scientists who study dolphins and with people who come to the center to learn about dolphins.

What will they share? So far, the team has learned that the calves that eat fish at an earlier age—not depending only on their mothers' milk—have a better chance of surviving.

Like the dolphin researchers, you've started your animal log with the frog. You will also use your log to record general observations on the fiddler crab and the land snail. Later in the unit, you can choose an interesting behavior you have observed and study it even further. Like Amanda and Karen, you can be an animal researcher, too.

A Day in the Life of the Study

On this morning, Amanda and Karen, members of the research team, go down to the dolphin lagoon. The lagoon is a natural saltwater habitat. Only a low fence separates the dolphins in their lagoon home from the open sea. Amanda and Karen sit on the dock next to where Cindy, a mother dolphin, and her baby are swimming. Amanda holds a data sheet. That's what she calls her animal log. Karen holds a stopwatch.

One of the things they're looking for is any baby dolphin "firsts," anything the baby is doing for the first time. What is the behavior between the mother and baby, and where is the baby? During a 15-minute period, Amanda and Karen repeatedly observe the dolphins for 10 seconds and then break for 20 seconds. They will come back to observe two more times today, once in the afternoon and once in the early evening. The observation times are **random;** they change from day to day. If Amanda and Karen see a behavior often, and at different times of day, they can get an idea of normal mother-calf behavior. Amanda, Karen, and the rest of the team will do this observing and recording every day for

Observing the Fiddler Crabs More Closely

Think and Wonder

The fiddler crabs have lots of interesting body parts to observe. What parts do the crabs use on land? What parts do they use in water? Let's take a closer look at the fiddler crabs.

Materials

For you

1 science notebook
1 **Record Sheet 6-A: Observing the Fiddler Crab**
1 **Record Sheet 6-B: Drawing the Fiddler Crab**
1 **Record Sheet 4-A: Observing the Frog**
1 hand lens
1 pencil
1 **My Habitat**

For you and your partner

1 orange-dotted cup with lid
1 fiddler crab

For you and your group

1 fiddler crab habitat
1 orange-dotted plastic spoon

Find Out for Yourself

1. Look at your crab observations from the last lesson. Then take out **Record Sheet 4-A: Observing the Frog.** Now that you've observed crabs, too, do you have more characteristics to add?

2. Add your list of frog characteristics to the first column of **Record Sheet 6-A: Observing the Fiddler Crab.** Do you see any characteristics on the chalkboard list to add to the record sheet?

3. Join your group around your crab habitat. Then collect your materials and begin to work.

4. Have you finished observing the crabs in their habitat? If so, ask your teacher to net a crab and put it into an "observing cup" for you.

5. Observe the crab up close in the cup. (It should be in the cup for just a few minutes.) Finish writing about and drawing the crab.

6. Talk about your observations with the other pair of students in your group. Also stick any new questions to the "What We Would Like to Know about Our Crabs" list.

7. Share your observations and drawings with the class. Then, put away your record sheets and clean up your materials.

8. You will work on the **My Habitat** sheet at home. What are some basic and special needs of humans? What is your habitat outside the school?

Ideas to Explore

1. Look at a map of the United States. See if you can find salt marshes and other wetlands near where you live. Would you find fiddler crabs in your area?

2. How is a fiddler crab like a spider? Do some research to find out.

3. Some people keep hermit crabs as pets. Do some research on hermit crabs. Would they make better pets than fiddler crabs? Why?

4. Do some research on salt marshes. How did people long ago use these marshes? How do people use them today?

Observing the Behavior of the Frogs and Crabs

Think and Wonder

You have thought a lot about the body parts of the frogs and crabs. But there's a lot to observe about what the crabs do. Today, you'll observe both animals some more. Early in the unit, the class asked some questions about the frogs and crabs. Which ones can you now answer?

Materials

For you

   1 science notebook

   1 pencil

   1 hand lens

   1 **Student Self-Assessment**

For you and your group

   1 dwarf African frog habitat

   1 fiddler crab habitat

Find Out for Yourself

1. Why is it important for you to observe the frogs and crabs some more before you get the snails? Discuss this with the class.

2. What behavior questions did you add to your animal log checklist? Do you have any questions about how to use your checklist and your log? Share your thoughts with the class.

3. Start working. Be sure to add any new questions to the class list.

4. Join your class for a science meeting. Share entries you have made in your animal log, **Science Discovery Sheets,** and record sheets. How do the frog and crab behave alike? How do they behave differently?

5. Share with the class any new ideas you have for the "Frogs" and "Crabs" lists.

6. Which questions can you now answer on the "What We Would Like to Know about Our Frogs" and "What We Would Like to Know about Our Crabs" lists? How could you learn the answers to the other questions? Share your thoughts with the class.

7. This is a good time to think about the work you have been doing. Fill out your **Self-Assessment.**

Ideas to Explore

1. Write a poem about your frogs or crabs.

2. When does a fiddler crab notice that you are coming near? Your teacher can tell you about a way to find out.

3. Do some research on the life cycle of the frog or crab. Your teacher can tell you how to make a life cycle wheel.

4. Pretend you are a frog or a crab. What is your life like? Write a story.

Living on Land: Snails

Think and Wonder

It's time to observe the third animal and to create its habitat. What goes in the land snail habitat? What does the land snail need to survive in the classroom? What questions do you have about snails?

Materials

For you
- 1 pencil
- 1 science notebook
- 1 hand lens

For you and your partner
- 1 land snail

For you and your group
- 1 tank with lid
- 1 piece of moss
- 1 cup
- 1 water mister
- 1 china marker
- 2 cups of moistened soil
- 1 cup of gravel
- 1 metric ruler
- Leaf litter

Find Out for Yourself

1. Look at the "Habitat Information Table." Share some observations about characteristics of the fiddler crab's habitat.

2. Look at your snail habitat proposal from Lesson 2. Do you have any changes to make? Share them with the class.

3. How do the materials in the classroom match the parts of the snail's natural habitat? Share your ideas with the class.

4. How should the materials be arranged in the snail habitat? Help the class think of the steps for building the snail habitat. The picture shows you what the habitat should look like.

Figure 8-1

Snail habitat

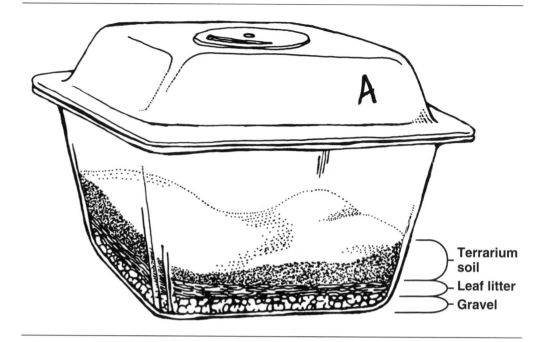

Terrarium soil

Leaf litter

Gravel

5. Help your group decide who will be the moderator, recorder, investigator, and reporter.

6. How do you collect the gravel and soil mixture? Pay attention as your teacher explains.

7. Get your materials for the snail habitat. Before you create the habitat, remind your group's recorder to list every living and nonliving thing that goes in the habitat.

8. Let your teacher know when you have finished creating the snail habitat. Observe the snails your teacher puts in the habitat.

9. Return all your materials (except the habitat) to the distribution center.

10. Do the snails have everything they need to survive in the classroom? Feed the snails. Then talk to the class about these questions:

    ■ What happened when you put food in the habitat?

    ■ Do the snails respond to food the same way the frogs or crabs do?

    ■ In what ways is the snail's response different?

11. Look at the circle your teacher has made. Listen as the group reporters share their lists of living and nonliving parts of the snail habitats.

12. Talk about caring for the snail with the class. It's important to remember these things:

    ■ **Air.** Tape the air dial on the lid in place. A small hole should let the air in, but not let the snails crawl out.

- **Water.** Feel the soil. If it is too dry, mist the soil lightly. If mold is growing, the soil is too wet. Then you need to remove the mold and let the habitat dry out a little. Twice a week, mist the moss only.

- **Food.** Feed the snails small pieces of lettuce, oranges, mushrooms, and apples every day. Take away old food to keep it from molding. Know when it is your group's turn to bring in food for the snails. Add more oyster shell as needed.

- **Temperature.** The snails will be active at a room temperature that does not go much below 15°C to 20°C (60°F to 68°F). They will move more on humid nights. They will move less at colder temperatures.

- **Habitat placement.** Keep the snails in indirect light or shade. Keep habitats out of extreme heat, drafts, and sunlight.

- **Waste matter.** After a few days, the snails will have left waste on the top of the habitat. Once in a while, rinse and dry the lid.

13. What questions do you have about the land snail? Write them down on note paper and initial the notes. Then tape them on the sheet called "What We Would Like to Know about Our Snails."

Ideas to Explore

1. Research different kinds of snails. Draw different shells of snails around the world.

2. Read books about life in forests, such as *One Day in the Tropical Rainforest*, by Jean C. George.

3. Which other animals have a shell? Read books such as *Creatures All Around Us—What's Under that Shell?*, by Dorothy Souza.

4. Invite a zookeeper, veterinarian, or pet store employee to your class. Ask them to tell you about what they do.

LESSON 9	# Observing the Land Snails More Closely

Think and Wonder

Today you'll take a closer look at the land snail. You'll draw it, too. When the snail moves, what does it leave behind? What else would you like to find out about land snails?

Materials

For you

- 1 science notebook
- 1 **Record Sheet 6-A: Observing the Fiddler Crab**
- 1 **Record Sheet 9-A: Observing the Land Snail**
- 1 **Record Sheet 9-B: Drawing the Land Snail**
- 1 hand lens
- 1 pencil

For you and your partner

- 1 land snail

For you and your group

- 1 land snail habitat
- 1 water mister
- 2 pieces of black paper
- Snail food

Find Out for Yourself

1. Take out **Record Sheet 6-A: Observing the Fiddler Crab.** Add any new kinds of characteristics from **Record Sheet 6-A** to **Record Sheet 9-A: Observing the Land Snail.**

2. Join your group around your snail habitat. Make sure you have hand lenses, a water mister, and paper towels.

3. Are your snails out of their shells? If so, observe them and work on **Record Sheets 9-A** and **9-B.**

Figure 9-1

*Guiding snails
as you observe*

4. Observe your snails even more closely. Here's what to do:

    ■ Carefully remove the lid of the habitat. Close the dial. Place the lid down on your table. It will be your observation tray.

    ■ Test the water in your mister to be sure it is warm. If not, replace it with warm water.

    ■ Mist the tray and create a small shallow puddle in one corner.

    ■ Place the snails in the puddle with the shell opening down in the warm water.

    ■ Keep watching. The snails should emerge in 5 to 10 minutes.

    ■ Keep the snails in the tray. If they are on the edge, gently guide them back in.

    ■ When you are done, put the lid back. Open the dial a little and retape it.

5. Put one piece of black paper on your table. Fold the other piece in half to make a "tent" to place over the first piece of paper. Put a snail on the flat piece of black paper. What happens after a snail crosses it? Be sure to record your observations.

6. Are you finished with both record sheets? Talk about your observations with your whole group. Also tape new questions to the "What We Would Like to Know about Our Snails" list.

7. Help the class compare the three habitats. Share your thoughts about these questions:

   ■ Are there any nonliving elements of the animals' habitats that affect their lives and that we should add to our lists?

   ■ Are there any important habitat elements missing from our lists?

8. Which living parts of the habitat do all three animals need? Which nonliving parts? Share your thoughts with the class.

9. Help the class add new snail information to the "Habitat Information Table."

Ideas to Explore

1. Write poems about snails.

2. Do you know what it means when an animal is "nocturnal"? Look it up. Are snails nocturnal? What other animals are nocturnal?

3. How slowly do your snails move from one point to another? What ways can you think of to measure snail movement? Can you figure out how many inches per minute (or miles per hour) the snail moves?

4. Research animals that could live in the same habitats as the frogs, crabs, and snails.

How Do the Animals Respond to a Change in Their Habitats?

Think and Wonder

What happens if you change the amount of light in each habitat? What will each animal do? Let's do an experiment to find out. Will any of the animals surprise you?

Materials

For you

1   science notebook
1   pencil
1   **Record Sheet 10-A: Our Investigation**

For you and your group

1   flashlight
1   dwarf African frog habitat
1   fiddler crab habitat
1   land snail habitat

Find Out for Yourself

1.   How does each animal behave every day? Review your logs to find out. Then discuss your ideas about these questions with the class:

     ■   When does each animal feed?

     ■   When is each animal most active? Least active? How do you know?

     ■   Where does each animal spend most of its time?

2.   Look at the list of habitat parts. There are both living and nonliving parts. How does each element affect each animal? Share your thoughts with the class.

3.   Which habitat parts could change? What if the amount of water changed? How might this affect each animal? Talk about these questions with the class.

4.   Look and listen as your teacher goes over **Record Sheet 10-A: Our Investigation.**

5. Remember, you will change the amount of light in each habitat. Help the class think of the steps in the experiment.

6. Decide who in your group will be moderator, investigator, recorder, and reporter. Then pick up your materials and start the experiment.

7. Are you finished with the experiment? Clean up and put your group's habitat back in its storage space.

8. What did your group predict? Why? Share your thoughts with the class.

9. Your group's reporter will share your experiment results with the class. Did any group get a different result from your group's? If so, why do you think so? Share your ideas with the class.

10. Think about each animal's response. Did it fit with your earlier observations of the animal's behavior? Discuss this question with the class.

Ideas to Explore

1. Observe how snails move on different surfaces. You can place one snail on a smooth surface and one on a rough surface. Time how quickly the snails move from one point to another.

2. Observe the behaviors of your pets at home. Keep an animal log on your pets and share your observations with classmates.

3. Read books about observing animal behavior, such as *Turtle Watch*, by George Ancona.

4. What happens when you do some other experiments with your animals? For example,

   - What happens when you move an object toward the animal?

   - What happens when you make a loud noise?

   - What happens when you put an obstacle in front of the animal?

   - How can you cause the animal to change its movement?

Observing Humans Closely

Think and Wonder

Today, you will talk about your home habitat. You will also discuss your school habitat. Which of your needs gets met in your home? Which of your needs gets met in your school? What do we mean when we say a habitat is "complete"?

Materials

For you

1 science notebook

1 **My Habitat**

1 copy of **Record Sheet 9-A: Observing the Land Snail**

1 copy of **Record Sheet 11-B: Observing Humans**

For you and your group

1 copy of **Record Sheet 11-A: My School Habitat**

Find Out for Yourself

1. Take out your home habitat study. Describe the things you do each day. These questions will get you started:

   ■ Where and how are your basic needs met in your home?

   ■ What are some of your daily activities?

   ■ Do you think your basic needs are met completely or partly in your home?

   ■ Where would you get food if the refrigerator was empty?

   ■ Where would you get water if the faucets did not work?

   ■ What needs to be brought into your home so that you can survive?

2. Did you list your neighborhood or town as your habitat? If so, tell the class why.

3. Help the class name all the living and nonliving things on the class web. Add any new things you can think of.

4. Look at the class web and discuss it with your group. Then fill out **Record Sheet 11-A: My School Habitat.**

5. Does the school completely meet your needs? Or, does the school partly meet your needs? Discuss these questions with the class:

   ■ Could we live in the school? Why?

   ■ How does the school meet your needs for food? Water? Shelter?

   ■ Is there enough space? Where might students sleep?

   ■ Is anything missing?

6. How long could you live in the school if nothing was brought in? Where would you get food if the cafeteria ran out? Share your ideas with the class.

7. What would need to happen for your home and school to become complete habitats? Explain your thoughts to the class.

8. Is the crab habitat complete? The snail habitat? The frog habitat? Share your ideas with the class.

9. Where in the school or at home could you observe humans? Fill out **Record Sheet 11-B: Observing Humans.** Use **Record Sheet 9-A** as a guide. What kinds of characteristics can you think of to observe?

10. Make a new section in your animal log. Use it to record observations of humans.

11. Share your observations of your classmates with the class. In what ways do humans vary?

12. Join the class for a science meeting. Why do you think humans can live in different places? Discuss these questions with the class:

   ■ Where do humans live? In what kinds of places?

   ■ In what ways do humans depend on their environment?

   ■ If you moved to Alaska (or Florida), how would you need to change the way you live?

   ■ How might your daily activities need to change?

13. Help the class add humans to the "Habitat Information Table." Discuss why some habitat parts have more than one answer. Also compare the information on humans with the information on the snail, crab, and frog.

14. Think about these questions:

   ■ In what ways do the crab, snail, and frog depend on their environments? How about humans?

   ■ In what ways do the crab, snail, and frog cause changes in their environments?

   ■ In what ways do humans cause changes in their environments?

Ideas to Explore

1. What if you were going to live for a long time all by yourself? What would you need to bring with you?

2. Go on a neighborhood habitat walk with the class. Where and how does the neighborhood help meet the needs of the humans who live there? What needs do the places on the route satisfy?

3. Read aloud and discuss a book about people who meet their needs in unusual ways, such as *Island of the Blue Dolphins*, by Scott O'Dell.

4. Make "people analogies"—for example, "Foot is to person as paw is to dog," or "Hand is to person as claw is to crab."

Researching Animal Behavior

Think and Wonder

You have observed lots of different behaviors of the frog, crab, and snail. Would you like to take a closer look at some behaviors? Before you can, you'll need to answer some questions. How often will you observe the behavior? What tools will you use? What will your log sheet look like?

Materials

For each student

1 science notebook

1 **Record Sheet 12-A: Animal Behavior Research**

Find Out for Yourself

1. How did the researchers at the Dolphin Research Center choose a specific dolphin behavior to study? Share your thoughts with the class.

2. Look over your animal log and the class list of what you think about each animal. What behaviors could you research some more just by observing? Share your thoughts with the class.

3. Help your class decide which behaviors you can and cannot study just by observing.

4. Remember the light experiment you did in Lesson 10? What made that a good science investigation? Share your thoughts.

5. Review **Record Sheet 12–A: Animal Behavior Research** with your teacher. Work with your research team to think of a behavior to study and a research question. Help fill out Section A of the record sheet.

6. Share your team's research question with the class. You may need to put it in different words to make it clearer.

7. Look and listen as your teacher goes over the "Planning" section of the record sheet.

8. Now work with your team on the "Planning" section of the record sheet. Ask your teacher to check your work when you are done.

9. Share the log sheet you and your team made. Decide how you want to record your animal observations. Share with the class what you will observe and why.

10. Look and listen as your teacher goes over the "Presenting Our Results" section of the record sheet. Think about what tools you would like to use to present your results.

Ideas to Explore

1. Write to a local zoo or college to find out if they are conducting animal behavior research. Find out what they are researching. What are their research steps?

2. Invite an animal behaviorist to visit your class. What questions will you want to ask?

3. Choose a human behavior to study. Or, if you have a pet at home, choose a behavior of that pet to research.

4. Write an article about your research for your school publication or class newsletter.

Part 1: What Makes an Animal Special?

Think and Wonder

Which body parts help humans find and eat food? How does human behavior help us survive in different habitats? Today, we'll take a closer look at human body parts and their jobs.

Materials

For you

1 pencil

1 science notebook

1 hand lens

Record Sheet 13-A: Humans—Structures and Behaviors

Completed **Record Sheet 11-B: Observing Humans**

Find Out for Yourself

1. Listen as your teacher explains what you will be doing over the next few lessons.

2. Review **Record Sheet 13-A: Humans—Structures and Behaviors** with the class. Then take out your completed **Record Sheet 11-B: Observing Humans** and your animal log observations on humans.

3. Review your work on the record sheet and animal log. Discuss these questions with the class:

   ■ Which body parts help humans find and eat food?

   ■ Which body parts help humans protect themselves? Hide from danger? Find or design and build shelter?

   ■ Which body parts help humans move around their habitats?

   ■ What other body parts do you think help humans survive?

   ■ How does the location, shape, or size of these body parts help the body parts function?

4. Work with the class to decide on a human structure to record on **Record Sheet 13-A.**

5. Now work with your group to record more body structures, their functions, and how they help humans meet their needs.

6. Share your ideas with the rest of the class.

7 What behaviors do you think help humans survive in a variety of habitats? Look over your animal logs to help you. Share your ideas with the class.

8. Now work with your group to identify more human behaviors. Record them on Record Sheet 13-A.

Ideas to Explore

1. Why do different peoples, such as the Inuit or northwest American Indians, show animals in their art? Do some research and report your findings to the class.

2. Start a nature journal. You can observe animals in your backyard or neighborhood. Share with the class ways animals are specially suited for life in these habitats.

3. Create alliterative poems or phrases to describe each animal. Figure 13–1 shows one example.

4. Find out the ways human hands are similar to and different from the hands of gorillas, chimpanzees, spider monkeys, and other primates.

Figure 13-1

Sample poem

Part 2: What Makes an Animal Special?

Think and Wonder

Which structures and behaviors help the frog, crab, and snail survive in their habitats? Today, you will have another chance to identify these things. But there are some animal facts you may not be able to observe right away on your own. Let's read about them.

Materials

For you

    1 pencil

    1 science notebook

    1 hand lens

    Completed **Record Sheets 4-B, 6-B,** and **9-B**

For you and your group

    1 frog habitat

    1 crab habitat

    1 snail habitat

    1 water mister

    Completed **Record Sheets 12-A** through **12-D**

Find Out for Yourself

1. Do you have any questions from your work in the last lesson? This is a good time to ask your teacher.

2. Your teacher will give you a record sheet. It will tell you which animal you and your group will focus on today. Follow these steps as you work:

    - Work in pairs. Use your notebook and animal habitat to help you.

    - Revisit your scientific drawing of the animal. Ask yourself, "Have I included the structures that help this animal survive in its habitat?" Then add to your drawing if you need to do so. On the bottom of the drawing, write a few sentences describing what you added to the drawing and why. If you chose not to add anything, explain why not.

■ When your group is ready, hold a science meeting. Select a group moderator and reporter. Share your work on the record sheet with each other. Be prepared to have the reporter explain in what ways your group thinks your animal is best suited for life in its particular habitat.

3. Have your group's reporter share your ideas with the class. You may volunteer to display your scientific drawing.

4. There are facts about your animals you might not have observed. Find out what they could be by reading "Did You Discover...?"

5. Share with the class your thoughts on the reading selection. What information in your animal log or record sheets supports things you have learned in the reading selection?

6. Write in your science notebook about one of these questions:

■ In what way(s) would the frog's life be changed if the frog did not have webbed feet? (You can choose a different animal and characteristic to write about.)

■ Imagine you are the frog, crab, or snail. How do you get what you need to survive? What structures and behaviors help make you best suited to life in the pond, marsh, or woods?

Ideas to Explore

1. Research the ways humans change their behaviors to live in different places on land, below the sea, and in space. How have humans needed to change to survive?

2. Compare the tools humans use for survival with nature's "tools" for animals. With the class, read a book such as *An Elephant Never Forgets Its Snorkel*, by Lisa Gollin Evans.

3. Read some poems about interesting creatures. Read from a book such as *Curious Creatures in Peculiar Places*, by Amy Goldman Koss, or *Voices of the Wild*, by Jonathan London. Then write a poem about a creature you find interesting.

4. What places in and around your school grounds or town have animals adopted as their shelters? With the class, read a book such as *Urban Roosts: Where Birds Nest in the City*, by Barbara Bash.

5. What other animals live in the habitats of the frog, crab, and snail? What structures and behaviors help these animals survive in their habitats? Do some research. How are these animals like and unlike the frog, crab, and snail? Present your findings to the class.

There's No Place Like Home

Think and Wonder

Could the frog survive in the snail's habitat? Could the crab survive in the frog's habitat? Could humans live in a marsh, pond, or woods? Today, you'll think about these questions. And, you'll read about one more animal: the beaver. What special behaviors do beavers have that help them survive in their habitats?

Materials

For you

1 pencil
1 science notebook
1 hand lens

For you and your group

1 frog habitat
1 crab habitat
1 snail habitat
Completed **Record Sheets 13-A** and **14-A, 14-B,** or **14-C**

Find Out for Yourself

1. Discuss these questions with the class:

   ■ What structures or behaviors reveal the greatest differences between the animals' lives?

   ■ What characteristics of the frog, crab, snail, and human will help us compare the ways they get what they need from their habitats?

2. Help your group decide who will be moderator, recorder, investigator, and reporter. With your group, record the structure or behavior your teacher gives you. Then, compare all four animals.

3. The reporters will share their groups' comparisons of the four animals. Then discuss these questions:

   ■ What is the job or function of each structure or behavior?

- In what ways are the animal's structures or behaviors similar? Different?

- Which differences help each animal survive in its particular habitat?

4. Write in your notebooks the answers to one of these questions:

   - Could the frog survive in the snail's habitat? Why or why not?

   - Could the crab survive in the frog's habitat? Why or why not?

   - Could the snail survive in the crab's habitat? Why or why not?

5. If you would like to, share your writing with the class.

6. Could humans live in a marsh, pond, or woods? Share your thoughts with the class.

7. Do you know much about beavers? Learn more by reading "What Makes Beavers Special?" (pgs. 53–55).

8. After reading, discuss these questions with the class:

   - What special characteristics do beavers have that help them survive in their habitats?

   - In what ways do beavers change their surroundings so that they can survive?

   - What other animals can change their surroundings so that they can survive?

Ideas to Explore

1. Create dioramas of the fiddler crab, land snail, or dwarf African frog in their natural habitats. Share your dioramas with younger children.

2. Put on a puppet show about the life of one of the animals you have studied. Stage the show for younger children.

3. See how different body structures affect different animals. Read books such as *Bizarre and Beautiful Eyes*, by Santa Fe Writers Group; *Heads*, by Ron and Nancy Goor; and *Breathtaking Noses*, by Hana Machotka.

Reading Selection

What Makes Beavers Special?

Look! Over there! Water is backed up behind a dam of sticks and mud. Pointed tree stumps stand along the water's edge. A mound of sticks floats in the middle of a pond. What do these signs tell us? This could be a beaver family's habitat.

Remember, a **habitat** is a place where an animal or a plant lives. Every animal has different needs for living. Most animals must find a habitat that meets these needs. But the beaver is different. The beaver is a lot like us. It finds a habitat and then changes it to suit its needs.

On Land and Water

Beavers live on land and in water. On land, beavers are clumsy. Their front legs are short. They cannot walk very fast. They cannot easily escape their enemies on land. But beavers are excellent swimmers and divers. In the water, they move quickly and gracefully.

Wolves and bears are the beaver's predators—they hunt and eat beavers. To keep its family safe, a beaver builds its home in the water. That home is called a **lodge.** The only way to get into the lodge is through an underwater tunnel.

Gnawed stumps

Pond

Food pile

Lodge

Main dam

Canal

Secondary dam

Why Build a Dam?

But what if the river or stream is too shallow to build a lodge? Rather than search for a different site, the beaver will build a **dam.** A dam holds back the water. To build the dam, beavers use their short front feet. They push mud, branches, and stones to create a ridge in the water. Then they use their sharp teeth to cut down trees.

Beavers cut down most of the trees near the water. Then they go into the woods for more trees. It is easier for beavers to move the heavy wood by floating it in water than by dragging it on land, so they dig **canals** in the ground. Water runs along the canals, which connect the wooded area to the pond. The beavers use the canals to float the logs down to the pond or river.

The beavers push the freshly cut sticks and logs into the muddy ridge they have created. Now the dam is complete. Water cannot flow above or around the dam. Soon the water in the stream forms a deep pond. And the beaver can build its lodge.

Step Inside . . .

From the outside, a beaver's lodge looks like a pile of sticks in the water. But inside, the beavers are dry and cozy. Inside their home, they build ledges above the water. The beavers sleep on the ledges, which are made out of sticks, wood chips, and grass.

Before winter comes, the beavers will add layers of sticks and mud to the lodge roof. The mud will harden and keep the lodge warm even in the coldest weather.

The beavers also collect extra sticks and leaves. These make a good food pile. Beavers keep the food pile in the water. They put it just below the tunnel that leads into the lodge. When the pond freezes, the beavers leave the lodge and swim to the bottom of the tunnel. They can eat from the food pile without leaving the water.

Keeping Warm and Dry

Like all mammals, beavers are warm-blooded and have fur. The outside layer of **guard hairs** are long and stiff. They protect the **underfur,** which is short and soft. The underfur traps air to protect the beaver against the cold and to prevent water from reaching the skin. A layer of fat under the fur also helps keep the beaver warm.

A beaver has glands on the bottom of its tail. The glands produce oil. The beaver puts the oil on its fur using a special "split toenail," located on the second toe of each back foot. The oil helps prevent the fur from absorbing water that can wet the beaver's skin.

Special Body Parts

A beaver has other special body structures that help it swim and work. Its back, or **hind,** feet are webbed like a duck's. They help the beaver move through the water.

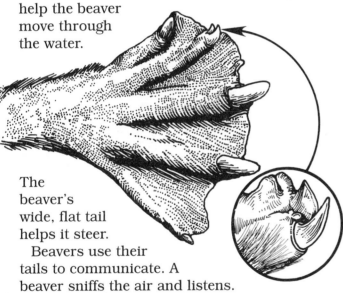

The beaver's wide, flat tail helps it steer.

Beavers use their tails to communicate. A beaver sniffs the air and listens. A fox is coming near. Whap! A beaver smacks its wide tail on the water's surface. Do you know why? All of the beavers in the area hear the warning and swim to the lodge for safety.

Beavers use their tails on land, too. The tail supports them like another leg. Beavers stand when they are cutting down trees. The tail helps them balance.

Like rats and squirrels, beavers are **rodents,** or gnawing mammals. A beaver has a hard orange coating on its two top and bottom front teeth. This coating keeps the teeth from chipping. There are two folds of skin behind the front teeth. These folds keep water out of the beaver's mouth while it gnaws on wood under water.

Have you ever used goggles in a pool? A beaver has its own built-in goggles. Each eye has a clear inner eyelid. This eyelid covers and protects the beaver's eye so it can see under water.

Beavers can stay under water for up to 15 minutes! Their lungs can hold a great amount of air. A beaver also slows down its heart rate when it dives. That way, it uses less oxygen when under water. A valve in the beaver's nose closes the nostrils while the beaver swims.

All of these characteristics help the beaver live in its habitat. Like humans, the beaver can change its environment more than most other animals on earth.

Presenting Our Research

Think and Wonder

It's time to share your research findings with the class. What did you learn about your animal's behavior? Did another team investigate the same question you did? Did it get the same results? You may not have been able to answer your research question. Does this ever happen to real scientists?

Materials

For you

1 completed **Record Sheet 12-A: Animal Behavior Research**

1 science notebook

Presentation materials

Find Out for Yourself

1. Discuss your results with another team that studied the same behavior of the same animal that you did.

2. After you have shared results, answer these questions in your notebook:

   ■ How did the way your team made its observations compare with the way the other teams studying the same animal or behavior made their observations?

   ■ Did another team's research give you any information that supports your observations? Why do you think so?

   ■ Did another team's research have different results from yours? If so, why do you think the results were different?

3. Now, share your team's results with the class. Be sure to talk about these things:

   ■ What your team's research question was

   ■ Whether the behavior was something you could observe

   ■ How many observation sessions you held

   ■ Some observations your team recorded

   ■ What conclusions you reached about the animal and whether these conclusions helped you answer your research question

■ What the team would do differently if it did this animal behavior research again and why it would do so

■ Any new question your team would like to research because of your experience

4. Does the behavior you have been studying help the animal survive in its habitat? Why or why not? Share your thoughts with the class.

5. Did your team answer its research question? Why or why not? Share your ideas with the class.

6. Now, think about how your research methods are like the methods used by the Dolphin Research Center you read about earlier (see pgs. 24–25). Then discuss your thoughts about these questions with the class:

■ What things most affected your research results?

■ Why do you think the Dolphin Research Center results might be more conclusive than your own research results?

Ideas to Explore

1. Read about animal behaviorists such as Jane Goodall, Konrad Lorenz, Karl von Frisch, Farley Mowatt, Niko Tinbergen, and Dian Fossey. Then outline the research methods the scientists used and compare them with the methods you used in class.

2. Research another interesting animal behavior, such as how the owl feeds. Visit the animal at a zoological park.

3. Find out if researchers are studying the behaviors of the fiddler crab, dwarf African frog, and land snail. Write to them. What can you learn about their studies? Compare your research results with the scientists' results.

4. On your school grounds, mark off a section in a field, woods, or vacant lot. Observe the animals in each section to discover some of their behaviors for survival.

Glossary

Abdomen: A segment of the body of many animals. The abdomen is the middle body segment of the fiddler crab.

Adaptation: A body structure or behavior that enables an animal to better survive or to reproduce; the process by which an organism changes.

Analyze: To study something by breaking it down into simpler parts.

Appendage: A structure that sticks out from an animal's body, such as a leg, a claw, or an antenna.

Arthropods: A group of animals that have jointed legs and outer skeletons.

Behavior: The way in which an organism responds to its environment.

Biodiversity: The numbers and kinds of organisms in a habitat.

Biosphere: Regions of the earth (including air, land, and water) that support life.

Calf (plural, calves): The offspring of certain animals, including dolphins.

Canal: A waterway made by humans.

Classify: To put things together because they share one or more properties.

Conclusion: A decision that is based on observations or on a study of data.

Constant: A condition that is not changed in a scientific experiment.

Controlled experiment: A scientific investigation in which one variable is changed and all the others are kept the same, or constant.

Crustaceans: A group of animals with a protective exoskeleton covering their bodies.

Dam: A barrier that controls the flow of water.

Data: Information, such as that gathered during an experiment.

Environment: Everything that surrounds an organism.

Ethogram: A list of abbreviations for observed behaviors; used by scientists to help answer a research question about animal behavior.

Evidence: Something that offers proof.

Exoskeleton: A hard outer shell that covers the bodies of certain animals, such as crustaceans.

Experiment: A procedure that is carried out to investigate a scientific question.

Habitat: The place where an animal naturally lives.

Hibernation: A state in which an animal rests or becomes inactive when the weather becomes extremely cold.

Hypothesis: A prediction about how something works or how two variables are related.

Instinct: Something that influences an animal's behavior but that does not have to be taught. For example, a snail digs holes to lay its eggs by instinct.

Lodge: A beaver's home.

Metamorphosis: A change in form or structure. Word used to describe the stages that an animal undergoes throughout its life cycle.

Mollusks: A group of animals with soft, unsegmented bodies and a protective shell. Snails and clams are mollusks.

Molt: To shed a skin or an outer layer.

Nocturnal: Relating to or happening at night.

Opinion: An expression of how one thinks or feels about something. An opinion is based on personal views, not necessarily on facts.

Organism: A living thing.

Pattern: A repeating arrangement of shapes, colors, numbers, or other things.

Plankton: Tiny forms of plant and animal life that float on water and are a source of food for aquatic animals.

Procedure: A series of steps that explains how to do something.

Property: Something about an object that helps identify it.

Random: Happening with no order or plan.

Reflex: An action that an organism takes automatically in response to stimulus; for example, quickly taking your hand off a hot lid.

Response: The reaction of an organism to a stimulus.

Rodents: A group of small animals with large, sharp front teeth that they use to gnaw things. Squirrels and mice are rodents.

Segmented: Divided into sections.

Stimulus: An outside influence that causes an organism to respond in some way.

Structure: The way in which the parts of an object or organism are arranged.

Variable: An element in an experiment that can be changed.